My Food, Your Food

Lisa Bullard

illustrated by Christine M. Schneider

M MILLBROOK PRESS · MINNEAPOLIS

For Grandpa B. —L.B.

For Grandma —C.S.

Millbrook Press
A division of Lerner Publishing Group, Inc.
241 First Avenue North
Minneapolis, MN 55401 USA

For reading levels and more information, look up this title at www.lernerbooks.com.

Main body text set in Slappy Inline 18/28.
Typeface provided by T26.

Library of Congress Cataloging-in-Publication Data

Bullard, Lisa.
    My food, your food / by Lisa Bullard ; illustrated by Christine M. Schneider.
        pages cm. — (Cloverleaf books. ™ Alike and different)
    Includes index.
    ISBN 978-1-4677-4903-9 (lib. bdg. : alk. paper) —
ISBN 978-1-4677-6031-7 (pbk.) — ISBN 978-1-4677-6293-9
(EB pdf)
    1. Food—Juvenile literature. 2. Diet—Juvenile literature.
3. Cooking, International—Juvenile literature. 4. Food habits—
Juvenile literature. I. Schneider, Christine, 1971– illustrator.
II. Title.
TX355.B926 2015
641.3—dc23   2014017246

Manufactured in the United States of America
1 – BP – 12/31/14

TABLE OF CONTENTS

Chapter One

It's Food Week!

Hi, I'm Manuel. My teacher, Ms. Chen, says we're learning about food this week. We each get to tell about **something special that our family eats.**

egg rolls

Tonight, Abuela is making a **tasty dinner.** *Abuela* means "Grandmother." She cooks the kind of food she grew up eating, first in Mexico and then in California.

Her burritos and salsa make my stomach happy!
Now I can't wait for my turn to talk on Friday.

Does your family have
a favorite dinner?

Chapter Two
Noodles from Different Places

spaghetti

Italy

At school on Tuesday, it's Tony's turn to talk. "My great-grandparents came here from Italy," he says. "My family loves **spaghetti** with **marinara sauce.** That's a kind of tomato sauce."

8

Ms. Chen tells us that people have moved to the United States from all over the world. They still make many of the foods from their home countries. Spaghetti and marinara sauce are Italian foods.

What parts of the world does your family come from? Do they like to eat any special foods from those places?

Ms. Chen shows us another kind of noodle dish. It's called yi mein. "Many cultures eat noodles," she says. "My parents moved here from China. They use **chopsticks** to eat their noodles."

China

Yi Mein

A cafeteria worker brings in plain noodles so we can try using chopsticks. Ms. Chen shows us how. **Noodles sure are sneaky!**

Chopsticks are very common in parts of Asia. Do you know how to use them?

Chapter Three

Flat Bread, Puffy Bread

On Wednesday, Marit and Raj share different breads. I can see that the breads are both flat and round like Abuela's tortillas.

Norway

India

Lefse

Roti

12

Raj's bread is called **roti**. His dad ate it growing up in India. It's chewy and good. Marit's bread is called **lefse**. It's from Norway. That's where her family comes from.

It melts in my mouth.

Then Lara shows us a braided bread called **challah**. It's puffy instead of flat. Lara's family is Jewish. They eat challah every Friday night. It's part of their religious tradition called **Shabbat**.

Ms. Chen tells us that many religions have traditions with food. For example, some people don't eat pork because of their religion.

Chapter Four

Families Make Different Choices

On Thursday, Jayla shows us her fishing pole. She tells us about fishing with her dad. They **cook** and **eat** the fish they catch.

"People have hunted and fished for food for thousands of years," Ms. Chen says.

She also says some families choose not to eat meat or fish. Others don't eat anything from animals. **That means no meat, eggs, or dairy products.**

Thursday after school, Abuela and I get busy in the kitchen. **We're making the food I'm going to talk about in school.**

Do you help your family cook meals? What food would you like to learn how to make?

Chapter Five

Finally, Friday

It's finally Friday. Have you guessed my food?
"**Salsa** is a Mexican sauce," I say. "Abuela and I make ours with tomatoes. I like it spicy."

Ms. Chen brought salsa for everyone. "There are tomatoes in lots of foods," she says. "Remember, they're in Tony's Italian marinara sauce too."

Here's what I learned this week: **even when food is different, it still can be alike!**

Make Your Own Salsa

Ingredients

1 can (28 ounces, or 794 grams) diced tomatoes
1 can (4 ounces, or 113 g) diced green chiles
2 green onions, thinly sliced

1 clove minced garlic
1 tablespoon lemon or lime juice
$\frac{1}{8}$ teaspoon salt
$\frac{1}{8}$ teaspoon pepper

Directions

**You can make salsa just like Manuel did! You'll
need an adult to help you with some tasks,
such as opening cans, chopping, and using a
blender.**

1) Wash your hands.

2) Drain the tomatoes. Set aside ¼ cup of the
tomato juice.

3) In a large bowl, mix together ¼ cup tomato
juice, drained tomatoes, and the other
ingredients. You can leave out the green
chiles if you don't like spicy food.

4) For chunky salsa, stir together and enjoy!

5) For smoother salsa, put everything into a
blender. Blend on the slowest setting for
just a few seconds. Continue blending a
few seconds at a time until the salsa is as
smooth as you like.

6) Serve the salsa with tortilla chips or with
Mexican dishes like tacos or burritos.

GLOSSARY

abeula: the Spanish word for "grandmother"

challah (HAH-luh): a braided Jewish bread

chopsticks: a pair of thin sticks used to eat with in many Asian countries

culture: the beliefs, foods, and activities shared by a group of people

dairy products: foods made from cow's milk, such as cheese and butter

Jewish: related to the religion called Judaism or to the people known as Jews

lefse (LEF-suh): a round, flat bread from Norway made with mashed potatoes and flour

marinara: a tomato sauce from Italy

religion: a set of beliefs in a god or gods

roti (ROH-tee): a round, flat bread from India and other southern Asian countries

salsa: a spicy sauce often made with tomatoes

tradition: a belief or way of doing something that has been passed down for many years

yi mein (YEE MAYN): a type of Chinese noodle dish

BOOKS

Ancona, George. *Come and Eat!* Watertown, MA: Charlesbridge, 2011.
Travel around the world to learn about different eating habits, celebrations, and foods.

Ichord, Loretta Frances. *Pasta, Fried Rice, and Matzoh Balls: Immigrant Cooking in America.* Minneapolis: Millbrook, 2006.
This book tells the story of how different immigrant groups brought food traditions to the United States.

Wagner, Lisa. *Cool World Cooking: Fun and Tasty Recipes for Kids!* Minneapolis: Scarletta, 2013.
Kid-tested recipes will teach you more about food from different countries.

WEBSITES

Easy Kids Recipes: International Recipes for Kids
http://www.easy-kids-recipes.com/international-recipes.html
Find easy recipes from around the world for you and your family to make.

USA for Kids: American Food
http://www.usconsulate.org.hk/pas/kids/food.htm
Learn more about American food, including Chinese American and Italian American foods.

LERNER e SOURCE™
Expand learning beyond the printed book. Download free, complementary educational resources for this book from our website, www.lerneresource.com.